BODY WORKS

CONTENTS

Introduction	2
Skeletons	4
Landlubbers	6
On the Wing	8
Aquatic Animals	10
Sound and Vision	12
Other Senses	14
Parts for Eating	16
Parts for Breathing	18
Brain Power	20
The Human Body	22
Glossary/Index	24

SCIENCE ALIVE

INTRODUCTION

Fish, birds, mammals, reptiles, and insects all look very different; yet they have at least one thing in common – body parts. Most types of animals have different parts for different functions, such as eating and breathing. Single-celled micro-organisms, however, carry out all the tasks needed for survival inside one cell.

Animals have specialized sens which make them aware of thin happening in their surrounding such as an approaching enemy, a sudden change in temperatur

Body structure also provides clu as to how an animal moves, as w as where it lives. Animal bodies displ great variety and degrees of complexi

2

SKELETONS

The shells of many insects, shellfish, and crustaceans are exoskeletons.

Jellyfish and caterpillars have fluid-filled hydrostatic skeletons.

Skeletons give support and assist movement. There are three main type Some of the smallest animals, such as micro-organisms, are supported by the pressure of a watery or jellylike material inside their bodies This is known as a *hydrostatic* skeleton

Insects and crustaceans, among other have hard *exoskeletons* on the outside their bodies. These rigid plates prote the animal against attack and dehydratio

Exoskeletons would be too heavy for larger animals. For this reason, reptiles, birds, ar mammals all have an internal skeleton made of bones, which resembles the suppor frame of a building. This is called an *endoskeleton*.

The bones of endoskeletons are slow to decompose, and more easily preserved than exoskeletons. By studying these bones, scientists can learn about species that lived long ago.

CONSTRUCTED SKELETON OF MOA BIRD

Moles have powerful front limbs and claws, which they use like shovels to dig tunnels.

LANDLUBBERS

L and-bound creatures have developed legs and feet of varying lengths and shapes. Fast-running animals, such as cheetahs and horses, tend to have long legs in relation to their body sizes.

Crocodiles and alligators have stubby legs. On land, they can travel quickly over short distances by raising their bodies. Some animals are designed for stamina, others for quick bursts of speed. Short limbs are often a sign of strength and digging ability.

Feet vary in size, and can have from one to five toes. Deer, antelope, and horses walk on the tips of their feet, which are protected by large nails or hooves. Other animals have claws, nails, and fleshy pads.

Some legless creatures, such as snakes, propel themselves along the ground using strong, circular muscles.

LEMUR

Lemurs, opossums, and spider monkeys have tails that can grasp and be used as extra limbs when climbing.

Ostriches are *ratites,* the name given to flightless birds. They use their wings like sails for steering and balance.

7

Bats are the only mammals with wings.

Beetles have hard, thick forewings to protect delicate flying wings when they are on the ground.

Sugar gliders have large flaps of skin between their front and back legs to help them glide.

ON THE WING

Moving in the air requires different body parts and shapes from moving on the land. Instead of pushing off the ground like land creatures, flying animals are designed to move against air. For this reason, the front limbs of birds and bats have developed into wings.

The design of a bird's wing is slightly curved from front to back, enabling the bird to pull upwards as it flies through the air. Bird skeletons comprise lightweight, hollow bones. As birds evolved, they lost unnecessary bones.

Insects can have either one or two pairs of wings. Butterflies move both sets of overlapping wings together at a slow rate, whereas bees and flies quickly dart. Flies hover in mid-air, as well as fly backwards.

Different wing shapes are used for different types of flight. The bald eagle glides on long, wide wings. Slots at the ends of the feathers can be opened and closed to allow it to take advantage of warm air currents.

The blue-footed booby has wings that pull back to give added speed as it dives for fish.

Birds that spend much time flying usually have lightweight, streamlined tails. Birds that live on the ground or in trees have developed tails that are shaped for uses other than flight. The red-shafted flicker uses its tail for balance when perching.

AQUATIC ANIMALS

Aquatic animals are adapted to life in a watery environment. Most of them have smooth, streamlined bodies which allow water to flow easily around them. Fish swim forward by flexing powerful muscles, and using side-to-side movements of the body and tail. Fins are used mainly for stabilizing, steering, and braking. Sea lions swim by moving their front flippers like oars. Frogs and ducks use their webbed digits like fins when in the water, and like feet when on land.

Octopuses and squid have a special way of swimming. They use a form of jet propulsion by sucking water into their bodies and then squirting it out to push themselves forward.

Sea urchins get about on moveable spines, and on their tube feet, which have suction cups on the ends.

SWIM-BLADDER

Fish can remain suspended effortlessly at any level in the water by making only minor adjustments to the amount of air in their swim-bladders.

Penguins swim by flapping their wings, which resemble flippers when under water.

Unlike most fish, stingrays seem to fly through the water by moving the sides of their bodies like wings.

SOUND AND VISION

Bats and whales locate prey by sending out a stream of sounds which bounce off objects as echoes. This is *echolocation*.

Some insects have hearing organs on their legs and antennae. A praying mantis has "ears" on its legs known as *tympana*.

Many animals view the world through a combination of sight and sound, smell, touch, and taste. Depending upon the particular animal, one of these senses may be more dominant.

Most animals need sight and hearing to communicate, detect food, and distinguish between the sounds of potential predators or prey. Young chicks still in their eggs can even communicate by making sounds from egg to egg to synchronize hatching. They fall silent when an adult gives an alarm cry. Most birds need the sense of sight to locate food, whereas a bat uses sound to "see". Bats crash into objects if their ears are covered.

Most spiders have eight eyes. The species that hunt for prey have much better vision than those that trap their prey in webs.

Mammals like deer and antelope, which are particularly at risk from predators, emerge into the world with well-developed eyes. Animals born in protected nests, like some bird species, don't open their eyes for several days.

13

OTHER SENSES

Otters hunting at night use their whiskers, or *vibrissae*, for feeling out food, such as fish and frogs.

Unlike most birds, the nocturnal kiwi has poor eyesight, so it locates food by smell. Its nostrils, at the end of its long beak, sniff out worms and other insects.

When sight is limited, such as in dark environments or at night, other senses become more important. Animals with poor sight or hearing often compensate with an acute sense of smell, touch, or taste. Nocturnal moths locate nectar by the scent of open flowers, while in the murky ocean, clams slam shut when they smell a predatory starfish.

Smell is also used for communicating. Cats scent-mark their territory, while insects like the silkworm moth send out an odour as a mating signal. Unlike the enormous variety of smells they can distinguish, animals can usually recognize only a few tastes, such as sweet and sour. Some animals have special "touch" cells on the ends of their whiskers or tentacles.

Fish experience taste not only in the mouth, but also in taste receptors in the gills and lips. Catfish have tactile "whiskers", with which they probe for food.

SILKWORM MOTHS

CLAM

A sea anemone has nerve cells on its skin surface which respond to light and dark, hot and cold, and acid and alkali.

PARTS FOR EATING

LION SKULL

DEER SKULL

BEAR SKULL

Jaws, teeth, and other body parts for eating have developed to suit particular diets. Sheep and other herbivores (plant-eaters) have long jaws, and strong, flat-topped teeth for grinding grass and leaves. Carnivores (meat-eaters), such as wolves, have sharp, pointed canine teeth, which they use to kill prey and rip flesh. Omnivores (plant- and meat-eaters) have a combination of both types of teeth.

What an animal eats also affects its digestive system. Most digestive systems contain bacteria to break down food. Many animals swallow food without attempting to chew it. Birds eat large chunks and store it in their *crop*, a chamber before their stomach.

Some aquatic animals, such as scallops, filter-feed by sieving out food from the water.

Snakes swallow their food whole, then digest it slowly over a few days.

The shape of a bird's beak provides a clue as to what it eats. Pelicans scoop up fish in their netlike bills, while parrots have hooked, nutcracker beaks.

PARTS FOR BREATHING

Fish gulp in water through the mouth and push it out over their gills to extract oxygen.

During their lifetime, frogs use more than one organ for respiration. As tadpoles, they breathe through gills. On land, mature frogs use lungs; but under water they "breathe" through thin skin, through which water can pass.

Most animals need to take in oxygen and give off carbon dioxide to survive. Land vertebrates, such as mammals, birds, and reptiles, use organs called *lungs* to breathe. Air passes down air tubes into air sacs, or *alveoli,* in the lungs. From here, oxygen seeps into the blood-vessels and is carried to other parts of the body.

Gills are the "lungs" of many aquatic animals, like fish and shellfish. Oxygen that is dissolved in water passes through the membranes of the gills and enters the blood.

Animals without lungs have special ways of breathing. Many insects have a system of tiny air tubes, or *tracheae,* near the surface of their skin.

One type of salamander, the Mexican axolotl, remains a tadpole all its life, and grows gills on the outside of its body.

Mammals that live in water, such as whales, have developed very efficient lungs. Some whale species can hold their breath for over 30 minutes.

The nostrils of the hippopotamus are positioned at the top of its head so that it can breathe with most of its head under the water. The animal can also block its nose when it fully submerges itself.

BRAIN POWER

APE

CAT

WORM

The brain acts as the body's control centre. In invertebrates, such as worms and insects, the brain is made up of small groups of nerve cells, or *ganglia*. These send impulses from the sense organs to the nerves. Vertebrates have a larger, more complex brain divided into three parts: the forebrain (cerebrum), midbrain, and hindbrain. Each part is developed to a different degree among animals, and is responsible for different functions.

Birds store the instructions for many instinctive behaviour patterns in their cerebrum. It is also the source of their abili to learn. Scientists make a distinction betwe animal *instincts* (the reflex reactions with which animals are born) and *intelligence* (t ability to learn from experience).

The red squirrel knows instinctively to bury nuts for a winter store, even when it has been raised in a cage on a liquid diet and has never seen nuts before.

Cheetah cubs have to learn how to hunt from watching their mother.

Primates have a huge capacity for learning. Koko was the first gorilla to learn sign language. Now she has a computer to talk for her. It has been specially designed with 70 pictures, or icons, to show the words that Koko uses often.

THE HUMAN BODY

Humans, too, are part of the animal kingdom. How do they fit into the picture? *Homo sapiens* (the scientific name for human beings) are vertebrates. The lower spine in humans is curved, which allows greater flexibility of movement than in most animals. People can run and climb, as well as co-ordinate more complex movements.

Sight is one of the most important senses for humans, but human eyesight is less developed than in most birds. Dogs have a sense of smell many thousand times greater than ours. The human body and its senses are generally less specialized than those of many animals. Its versatility, however, has enabled people to live in many different environments.

The human spine is unlike any other animal's backbone because humans are the only mammals to walk primarily in an upright position on two legs. This leaves the hands free for other tasks.

The human jaw and voice-box, together with parts of the mouth and throat, allow people to talk. However, it is the human brain that gives people the ability to communicate through language.

Opposable thumbs enable people to make and hold things with their hands.

NASAL CAVITY

TONGUE

JAW

VOCAL CHORDS

VOICE-BOX, OR LARYNX

GLOSSARY

alveolus – any of the many tiny air sacs in the lungs which bring air into contact with the blood

carnivore – an animal which eats other animals

cell – the basic unit or building block of a living organism

crop – a chamber in the gullet of many birds in which food is stored before digestion

crustacean – an animal without a backbone, and with a hard, crustlike covering, such as a crab or lobster

echolocation – a navigation system, based on sound waves. Animals emit sounds, which bounce off objects and return as echoes.

endoskeleton – an internal skeleton made of bone or cartilage

exoskeleton – a protective outer covering, like the shell of a crustacean

ganglion – any of the many nerve-cells which form the brain in some invertebrates

gill – the organ that fish and other aquatic animals use for breathing

herbivore – an animal which eats plants

hydrostatic skeleton – a fluid-filled support structure

instinct – a pattern of behaviour with which an animal is born

intelligence – a pattern of behaviour which an animal has to learn

lung – the organ that land-dwelling vertebrates, as well as some molluscs, use for breathing

nocturnal – describes animals which are active, or plants which open, at night

omnivore – an animal which eats both plants and animals

ratite – a bird that can't fly

swim-bladder – an air-filled sac in some fish, which they can adjust to allow them to easily move up and down

trachea – one of the air tubes through which an insect breathes

tympana – a thin membrane used by some insects to hear, usually located on the thorax or forelegs

INDEX

antennae	12
beaks	14,17
bills	17
bones	4-5,8,22
brains	20,23
cells	2,14-15,20
claws	6
crops	16
digestive systems	16
ears	12
eyes	12-13,14
feet	6,10
fins	10
flippers	10-11
gills	15,18-19
jaws	16,23
legs	6,8,12,22
limbs	6-7,8
lungs	18-19
mouths	15,18,23
muscles	6,10
nails	6
nostrils	14,19
shells	4
skeletons	4-5,8,22
skulls	16
spines	10,22-23
stomachs	16
swim-bladders	11
tails	7,9,10
teeth	16
thumbs	23
tympana	12
voice-boxes	23
whiskers	14-15
wings	7,8-9,11